THIS COLORING BOOK
BELONGES TO

Thanks For Start A Beautifull Journey With Us
It Is Our Wish That, Many
People Have Been Able To Realize
Their Imagination With Our Instructional Product

Don't Forget To Share Your
Love As A Reivew
On Our Product